THE SURVIVAL HANDBOOK

A Manual for the Survival Lifestyle

Written by Arya Skyee

Copyright Page

This book is based on the lived experiences and reflections of the author. It is intended for literary, educational, and awareness purposes only. It should not be considered therapeutic, diagnostic, or professional mental health advice. Readers who may be

 affected by trauma, addiction, or abuse are encouraged to seek support from qualified professionals or crisis services in their region.

Names, identifying details, and circumstances have been altered where necessary to protect privacy.

First Edition 2025
Printed in Canada

For permissions, inquiries, or media requests:
Empower Publishing

ISBN 978-1-0696536-7-3

Publisher's Note

Empower Publishing

The Survival Handbook: A Manual for the Survival Lifestyle is more than a book. It is a record of truth, written by one who lived it.
Every page challenges the narratives that have erased survivors of addiction, violence, and poverty for generations.

This work belongs to the people who were never meant to have a voice. It stands as testimony for those who have been judged by their survival rather than understood by their humanity.

At Empower Publishing, we believe stories like this are not tragedies they are evidence of endurance.
They remind the world that strength does not always look clean or quiet. Sometimes it looks like survival.

Dedication

For everyone who ever had to survive when the world looked away.
For the ones who did what they had to do and still carry the guilt.
For the women and men who lived by instinct because no one taught them safety.
For the children who learned to read danger before bedtime stories.
For the ghosts who did not make it out.
This book is for you.
You were never weak. You were adapting.

Table of Contents

Preface:

Survival is a lifestyle.
It is a heartbeat that refuses to stop even when your world does.

Some of us were not raised in safety. We were raised in reaction. We learned how to move before we were seen and how to read danger before it spoke. We were taught that love is inconsistent, that money is faster than healing, and that trust is a luxury for people who never had to fight for their next meal.

This is not a recovery book.
It is not even a redemption story.
This is the psychology of the streets. It is the unspoken truth of addiction, the loyalty code of the trade, and the emotional structure of people who live by instinct.

People like us.

The survival lifestyle is not something you choose. It chooses you when the world stops offering choices. It molds you. It hardens you. Then it dares you to find your soul again inside the wreckage.

This book is my story but it is also yours. If you have ever stolen to eat, loved someone who broke you, or looked in the mirror and wondered who you had to become just to make it through the night, you belong here.

This is not about shame. This
is about truth.

Prologue

There are two kinds of people in this world.
Those who survive and those who never had to.

This book is not about healing.
It is not about redemption or forgiveness.
It is about survival.
The kind that does not look pretty or make sense to people who were never forced to live it.

Survival has its own language.
It speaks in hunger and silence.
It moves through alleyways and motel rooms.
It breathes in spaces where love and fear sound the same.

Some people read about the streets.
Others are raised by them.
This is not a story meant to impress or inspire.
It is a record of what it costs to stay alive when the world stops giving you choices.

Every chapter that follows was written from the place between fight and surrender.
From the high that feels like heaven and the morning that feels like hell.
From the loyalty that keeps you breathing and the betrayal that takes your last breath.

If you came here looking for recovery, you will not find it.
If you came here looking for truth, you already know it.
This book is for the ones who have been there.

The ones who have seen the game, lived the hustle, tasted the fall, and still woke up breathing.

Because sometimes surviving is not the beginning of a new life. It is just proof that the old one could not kill you.

Chapter One: The Hustle

The hustle is not a job.
It is a heartbeat.
It is the sound of my footsteps on cold pavement, chasing money, chasing escape, chasing breath. It is the rhythm of panic mixed with purpose.
It is what happens when the world gives you nothing and still expects you to survive.

I learned early that love could hurt worse than hunger. That being born into chaos means learning how to outthink danger before you can even spell it.
My first lessons in survival were not in classrooms. They were in the quiet moments between fear and reaction. When to speak. When to run. When to lie. When to make something out of nothing.

The hustle started for me long before I ever touched a drug or made a deal.
It started the day I realized no one was coming to save me.
I was young but already older than most grown adults I knew.
I had seen things that silence itself could not hold. And so
I learned to build a world I could control.

I became whoever the moment required.
The girl who could sell her pain with a smile.
The woman who could calm a man's storm before he broke everything in the room.
The fighter who could walk into any space and own it, even if my knees were shaking under the table.
You learn quick that control is not power. It is protection.

Addiction found me in the quiet.

Not in the streets at first but in the silence after them.
It was never about the high. It was about the pause.
That moment when everything inside me stopped screaming.
Drugs gave me peace before I ever found it sober. And
that is what made them dangerous.

There were nights I slept beside people I did not trust just to feel
safe.
There were mornings I woke up in houses that were not homes.
I stole to eat. I sold what I had to keep moving.
And still, I told myself I was fine.
Because in the survival lifestyle, "fine" means alive.

The streets teach you loyalty and betrayal at the same time. You
learn who will really ride for you when there is nothing left to gain.
You learn that family is not always blood and blood is not always
family.
You learn that forgiveness is expensive and pride is free but costs
everything.

There is pride in the grind.
A strange honor in being the one who always finds a way.
I told myself that if I could survive this, I could survive anything.
But survival is not the same as living.
Living means feeling again.
And after years of survival, feeling is the scariest thing in the
world.

The hustle taught me how to read people before they spoke. It
taught me how to move through any room like I belonged there.
It taught me how to rise again and again.
But it also taught me how to disappear.
How to pretend.

How to hide behind strength so no one saw how tired I was.

The hustle saved my life more times than I can count.
And it almost took it too.
But every time I fell, something inside me still whispered to get up.
To rise again.
To not let the streets have the final word on my story.

And that is where this handbook begins.
Not with the glory. Not with the grind.
But with the truth that I was never meant to just survive. I
was meant to rise.

"The hustle gives you the illusion of control.
But the truth is, the game is already studying you back." That
line sets up The Game perfectly and gives the reader the sense
that the story is about to turn darker and smarter.

Chapter Two: The Game

The game is not just the streets.
It is every system that feeds on struggle.
It is survival disguised as choice.
You think you are playing to win, but most of the time you are
only trying not to lose.

The game teaches you that everything has a price.
Time. Trust. Truth.
Every favor becomes a debt.
Every secret becomes a weapon.
And love becomes the most dangerous currency of all.

When I first stepped into the game, I thought I had power.
I knew how to talk my way into a room.
I knew how to make people feel seen.
I knew how to use what I had to get what I needed. But what
I did not see was how the game was studying me back.

There were men who smiled like safety and spoke like danger.
There were nights when I looked powerful and mornings when I
felt invisible.
The world clapped for my strength but never asked what it cost me.
They called it hustling.
I called it staying alive.

Addiction and the game walk hand in hand.
You tell yourself you can quit anytime, that you are in control.
But control is a lie that keeps you breathing.
The drugs, the men, the money, the rush they all feed the same
hole inside you.
The one that started long before the first high.

There was a time when I thought I was untouchable.
I was sharp, fearless, always one step ahead.
I knew who to trust for a night and who to never trust at all.
I could read a room before I walked in.
I could make chaos look like confidence.
But what no one saw was how broken I was beneath the armor.

The game rewards your pain when you turn it into profit.
It claps when you survive.
It punishes you when you feel.
So, I stopped feeling.
I learned how to shut off my heart and move like a shadow.

There were deals made in silence.
There were choices I still see when I close my eyes.
I learned how to lie to myself better than anyone else could.
I told myself I was strong when I was just numb.
I told myself I was free when I was chained to the life I built.

And yet even inside the madness, there were moments of grace.
The quiet kindness of strangers who did not know my story.
The friend who shared her last meal.
The client who looked at me and saw a human being instead of a service.
The rare nights when I could breathe without fear.

The game teaches you strategy.
It teaches you control.
But it does not teach you peace.
Peace is not something you can earn.
Peace is what you find when you finally stop running.

I learned that power without purpose is poison.
That being feared is not the same as being respected.
That survival without soul is just another kind of death.

The game gave me stories that most people would never believe.
It gave me scars that no one will ever see.
But it also gave me vision.
Because once you have seen how the game works, you can never unsee it.
And when you stop playing it, you start rewriting the rules.

That is where freedom begins.
Not when the world changes, but when you stop letting it define you.

"The game doesn't just sell drugs. It sells relief.
And that is the most expensive product of all."

Chapter Three: The Addiction

Addiction is not about drugs.
It is about relief.
It is about finding something that quiets the noise long enough to
remember what silence feels like.

My first high was not from a substance.
It was from escape.
That moment when pain finally shut up for a second.
When I did not have to feel like a mistake or a burden. When I
felt safe even if it was a lie.

The first time I used, I thought I found peace.
The world stopped spinning.
My body felt light.
I could breathe again without the weight of memory crushing my
chest.
And for the first time, I thought, this must be what normal people
feel like.

Addiction creeps in like comfort.
It never announces itself.
It does not knock on the door and ask for permission. It
just moves in and starts rearranging your life.

Soon it becomes your best friend and your worst enemy.
It tells you it understands.
It tells you it will never leave.
It tells you that you do not need anyone else because it will
always make you feel better. Until it doesn't.

For me, addiction became my identity.
I built my routines around it.
My people revolved around it.
My thoughts worshipped it.
It was the one constant in a world that kept betraying me.

I have lost count of the mornings I woke up promising it would be the last time.
The guilt sits on your chest heavier than withdrawal.
The shame seeps into your bones.
And yet, somehow, you still reach for it again because the pain of stopping feels worse than the pain of continuing.

There were moments when I tried to get clean and the world looked too bright.
The air hurt.
The silence screamed.
Sobriety felt like standing naked in a burning room. And people said it was strength, but I knew it was survival all over again.

Addiction was not just the drug.
It was the attention.
The chaos.
The routine.
The belonging.
Every hit or fix was just a symptom of something deeper that had never been treated.

I have used to forget love.
I have used to forget loss.
I have used to stay awake because nightmares felt too real.
And I have used to fall asleep because reality felt too heavy.

People like to talk about rock bottom like it is one single place.
It is not.
It is a series of floors that keep collapsing until you finally stop trying to stand on them.
For me, rock bottom was the day I realized I was not scared of dying anymore.
I was scared of living like this forever.

That is when I understood that recovery is not about being clean.
It is about being honest.
It is about looking at every version of yourself you tried to bury and saying, I still love you.
Even now.
Even here.

Addiction taught me that pain is not weakness.
It is information.
It is the body saying something needs to change.
And healing starts the moment you stop trying to numb it and start listening to it instead.

My story is not about perfection.
It is about persistence.
It is about finding meaning in the mess and grace in the relapse.
It is about remembering that even in the darkest rooms, the soul still knows where the light switch is.

Chapter Four: The Streets Raised Me

The streets did not just teach me.
They raised me.

They fed me when I was hungry and hurt me when I got too comfortable.
They gave me everything I thought I wanted and took everything I actually needed.

When I say the streets raised me, I mean they became my family when my own family broke apart.
They taught me loyalty before I even understood love.
They taught me silence before I learned safety.
They taught me how to smile through pain because weakness was blood in the water.

I remember sleeping in cars that were not mine.
I remember running from cops and men at the same time. I remember thinking if I could just make it through the night, the morning would be different.
It never was.
The streets do not forgive. They reset.

You learn early that there are rules no one writes down.
You show respect even when you hate someone.
You never snitch no matter what it costs.
You keep your word even when it breaks you.
You protect your people even if they would not do the same for you.
It sounds like honor, but it is really survival wrapped in code.

The first time I saw violence up close I was too young to understand it.
But the noise never left me.
It echoed in every argument after that.
Every fight.
Every time I raised my voice it was that sound coming back to life.

There were good moments too.

The laughter that came from nowhere.

The nights around kitchen tables counting money that felt like freedom.

The smell of cheap smoke and cologne mixed with the sound of loyalty.

Those moments made it easy to believe that maybe we were a family.

Maybe the streets could fill the hole that home left behind.

But the streets do not love you back.

They only mirror what you put in.

They use your pain as proof of strength.

They cheer for you when you rise and they circle when you fall.

There were nights I was chased through alleys with fear in my throat.

There were days when I played fearless while shaking inside.

There were people I called brother who disappeared overnight.

People I buried who never made it to twenty five.

And somehow, every time someone died, we just kept moving like it was normal.

I learned how to talk my way out of danger.

How to charm men who wanted power over me.

How to pretend to love them so they would not hurt me.

How to keep my hands steady when my heart was shaking.

The streets gave me that kind of education.

I used to believe the streets were the only place that understood me.

Because they never asked me to be clean or quiet.

They accepted me as I was.

Broken. Fierce. Hungry. Alive.
But the truth is they only mirrored the chaos I already carried inside.

The streets raise you to be tough.
But toughness comes with a cost.
You lose softness.
You lose trust.
You lose the part of you that still believes in good people.

There came a point when I looked around and realized everyone I called family was just surviving too.
We were all pretending to be fine.
We were all hiding the same pain behind different faces. And that was when I knew it was time to leave.

The streets made me who I am.
But they do not get to decide who I become.

Chapter Five: Love and Survival

Love and survival do not speak the same language.
Love whispers.
Survival shouts.
Love wants peace.
Survival wants proof.
When you grow up in chaos, you learn to read danger before you ever learn to receive love.
You mistake intensity for intimacy.
You mistake control for care.
You mistake being chosen for being safe.

My first experiences with love were not gentle.
They were loud and fast and full of fire.
I thought love was supposed to burn because everything else in my life already did.
I thought the fighting meant passion and the silence afterward meant forgiveness.
I did not understand that love without safety is not love at all.

I found comfort in people who reminded me of my pain. I was drawn to the ones who could break me because breaking felt familiar.
It felt like home.
When someone treated me with kindness, I did not trust it. I waited for the catch, the shift, the punishment that always followed peace.

There were moments when love felt like survival.
The kind of connection that keeps you breathing even when you know it is killing you.
I stayed in places I should have run from.
I protected people who destroyed me.
I called it loyalty when it was really fear of being alone.

I thought if I could just love harder, it would fix them.
If I could just be enough, they would finally choose me in the right way.
But love is not earned through suffering.
Love does not grow in chaos. It
rots there.

I have been hit, silenced, manipulated, and forgiven too quickly.
I have forgiven things that still echo in my chest. I have looked in the mirror and apologized to the person who hurt me.

Because that is what survival does.
It teaches you to take the blame so you can stay alive.

Leaving is not the hard part.
Staying gone is.
Because survival makes you miss the very thing that almost killed you.
You start to crave the highs and lows, the push and pull. You confuse emptiness with love leaving the room.

But the truth is, love is not supposed to feel like war.
Love is not supposed to make you forget who you are.
Real love is quiet.
It does not rush.
It does not demand.
It waits for you to meet yourself again.

Healing taught me that love without boundaries is bondage. That I cannot save anyone who refuses to save themselves. That I am not hard to love, I was just taught by people who did not know how.
There are still days I catch myself flinching at kindness. Still nights when I miss people who hurt me because pain feels like home.
But every time I choose peace over chaos, I take another step toward real love.
Love that is not survival. Love
that is freedom.

"Love can chain you harder than the streets ever could.
And sometimes freedom costs more than captivity." It makes the reader feel the transition from emotional entrapment to the slow unraveling of control.

Chapter Six: The Cost of Freedom

Freedom sounds beautiful until you earn it.
Everyone talks about getting out, but no one tells you what it costs to stay gone.

Leaving the life is not one decision. It is a thousand small ones that break you open again and again.
You do not just quit the drugs or the streets or the chaos. You quit the version of yourself that knew how to survive there. And that is the hardest part.

The first days of freedom are quiet in a way that hurts.
You start to notice how loud peace really is.
There are no sirens, no drama, no constant alerts.
Just silence.
And that silence can feel like death when you have lived your whole life on adrenaline.
I remember waking up in the first safe place I had been in for years.
No locks on the door. No fear in the air.
And still I lay there wide awake, heart pounding, waiting for something to go wrong.
That is what freedom feels like when you have been caged too long.
It feels unsafe at first.

The detox was not just from substances.
It was from people, habits, survival patterns, and identities.
It was from the rush of danger and the illusion of control.
My body shook for days.
My mind screamed for chaos. Peace
felt like withdrawal.

There were moments when I wanted to go back because at least the pain there made sense.
At least I knew the rules.
At least I knew who I was.
Freedom forced me to face the person I had become, not the one I pretended to be.

Starting over meant learning how to live without the armor.
How to trust food in the fridge.
How to breathe without looking over my shoulder.
How to say no and mean it.
How to rest without feeling lazy.

It was humbling.
No one claps for you when you are healing.
There are no awards for staying sober, for rebuilding credit, for surviving court dates or custody battles.
But those are the real victories.
The kind that no one sees but you.

Freedom is not free.
It costs every piece of comfort you found in your pain.
It costs the friends who are not ready to rise with you.
It costs the identity that once kept you safe.
It costs you the illusion that survival is enough.

But freedom gives you something back too.
It gives you mornings that do not begin with panic.
It gives you nights that end in peace instead of fear. It gives you the chance to build a life that does not depend on pain to feel alive.

I learned that peace is not boring.

It is rare.

It is sacred.

It is what you fight for when you finally get tired of fighting everything else.

Freedom is not about running from your past.

It is about walking toward yourself.

It is about reclaiming your story, not rewriting it. Because every scar, every relapse, every mistake was still movement.

And movement is what healing looks like when it is real.

Chapter Seven: Straight Survival

Survival is not pretty.

It is not the glossy story people want to hear after you make it out.

It is teeth and hunger.

It is doing what you have to do even when it makes you hate yourself later.

Survival means finding food however you can.

It means borrowing money you cannot pay back. It means lying to people who care about you because the truth would make them leave.

It means sleeping next to danger and calling it safety because at least you are not alone.

There were nights I did not know where I would sleep.

Sometimes it was a couch.

Sometimes it was a floor.

Sometimes it was a stranger's bed.

You stop caring about comfort when you are chasing warmth.

Survival turns your body into currency.

You learn to smile when you want to scream.

You learn to act like you are in control when you are praying no one notices how scared you are.

You learn to read every room like it is a battlefield.

There were days I went without food so I could afford what kept me numb.

There were nights I sold parts of myself that no one had the right to buy.

You tell yourself it is just one time.

Then one time turns into a life.

And soon you are not even sure who you were before it started.

People like to ask, why did you not just leave?

As if survival is a choice.

As if you can walk away from the only life that ever made sense.

The truth is, leaving is not the hardest part. Believing you deserve better is.

Survival means hustling until your body gives out.

It means trusting people you should run from.

It means learning to lie so well that you start to believe it. It means loving people who use you because you need someone to need you.

There is no schedule in survival.

Days and nights blur together.

You count time by moments of fear and relief.

You measure success by whether you made it through without catching a charge, losing a friend, or losing your mind.

You learn how to make yourself invisible when the world is looking for someone to blame.

You learn how to fight with words when your fists are tired.

You learn how to beg without sounding like you are begging. You learn that pride will starve you if you let it.

I have eaten food I found in dumpsters.

I have walked barefoot in winter because my shoes were gone.

I have slept in bathrooms and alleys.

I have laughed in moments that should have broken me.

Because even in the worst of it, I still wanted to feel alive.

Straight survival is not about strength.

It is about instinct.

It is about a body that refuses to die even when the mind has given up.

It is about waking up one more day when you have no reason to.

People think survival is something to be proud of.

It is not pride. It is proof.

Proof that I made it.

Proof that pain does not mean defeat.

Proof that even in the dark, I kept breathing.

Chapter Eight: The Hustle Never Sleeps

The hustle does not stop when you do.

It keeps moving in your head even when you are standing still.

You can leave the streets but the streets do not leave you.

The hustle gets in your blood.

It becomes the way you breathe, the way you think, the way you move through every space.
You start scanning every room without meaning to.
You size up people by their shoes, their eyes, their tone. You see angles before you see faces.

Even when I got clean, my mind was still running like a trap house.
Every thought had a price tag.
Every move was a calculation.
Every moment of peace felt suspicious.

The hustle keeps you awake.
You cannot rest because rest feels like danger.
You cannot relax because relaxing gets you caught.
You keep grinding because slowing down feels like dying.

It is not ambition. It is conditioning.
When you live in survival long enough, chaos becomes your comfort zone.
You do not know how to live without pressure.
You chase stress because peace feels like withdrawal.

I have sat in clean apartments with money in my account and still felt broke.
I have checked the locks three times before bed even when I knew I was safe.
I have kept my phone close like a lifeline even when no one was calling.
Because the hustle never lets you forget what it took to get here.

There is a rush in the game that regular life cannot match.
The way your heart pounds when the deal goes through.
The way the money folds warm in your pocket.

The way the night smells like freedom and fear mixed together. That is a high that no rehab can detox.

But what no one tells you is that the hustle will drain your soul long after it stops paying your bills.
You start to feel empty in the quiet.
You start missing the noise that once broke you.
You start craving danger just to feel something again.

I have tried working regular jobs.
Clocking in. Clocking out.
Smiling when people say they are tired after a full shift. They do not know tired until they have been awake for days making survival look easy.

The hustle never sleeps because the fear never sleeps.
Even when you are safe, the memory of hunger is louder. Even when you are free, the sound of running is still in your bones.
You keep moving because stopping feels like a setup.

There is no o switch for survival.
You just learn how to channel it into something else. But the truth is, even when life is calm, the streets are still whispering.
Asking if you remember who you were.
Asking if you still got it.

And sometimes, when the night is quiet and the world feels too normal,
I do.
I remember the rush.
I remember the danger. I remember the version
of me that could survive anything. And I almost miss her.

Chapter Nine: Loyalty and Betrayal

Loyalty is the only religion the streets ever taught me.

It was the one rule that meant something.

You stay solid. You protect your own. You never talk. You never fold.

But loyalty in the game is a coin with two faces.

On one side is love.

On the other side is fear.

You never really know which one people are offering until it is too late.

I learned early that loyalty can kill you faster than betrayal. You stay with people who use you because you do not want to be another name they curse when you leave.

You take charges that are not yours.

You keep secrets that rot your spirit.

You call it loyalty when it is really survival in disguise.

There were people I would have died for.

People who said they would ride for me too.

Until the night came when everything went wrong and I learned that loyalty has an expiration date when fear shows up. The same mouths that swore they loved me were the first to go silent.

In that world, betrayal is not always loud.

Sometimes it is a whisper in a backroom.

Sometimes it is a deal you never knew was made. Sometimes it is a look that tells you the plan changed and you were not invited.

I have been betrayed by friends, lovers, blood.

People I fed. People I trusted.

And each time I told myself I was done believing in anyone. But then the next storm came and I reached for someone again because loneliness is a heavier burden than betrayal.

The code says you never snitch.
You never break.
You take the fall with silence and pride.
But no one tells you what it feels like when you are the only one still standing on that code.
No one tells you how it breaks you to realize loyalty is not contagious.

I kept giving my loyalty to people who did not earn it because it was all I had to give.
It was my proof that I was still human in a place that tried to make me forget.
Even when the world betrayed me, I refused to become like it. That was my rebellion.

There was a man I trusted with my life.
He had the kind of smile that made you feel safe and the kind of eyes that saw too much.
We made money together. We survived together.
But when things got heavy, he disappeared.
Left me holding the weight of both our choices. That was the day I learned that loyalty and love are not the same thing.
I forgave more than I should have.
Because forgiveness felt like control.
It was easier to forgive than admit I had been fooled again. It was easier to stay loyal to ghosts than start over alone.

Betrayal does not just break trust.
It rewires it.

After a while, you start watching everyone like a threat.

You stop expecting truth from anyone.

You keep people close enough to use them but far enough that they cannot use you first.

That is what survival does.

It makes your heart a vault.

It makes your loyalty conditional even when you pretend it is not.

You keep giving pieces of yourself hoping one of them will stay.

The streets taught me that loyalty is not about words.

It is about consistency when no one is watching.

And betrayal is not always hate.

Sometimes it is fear dressed as love.

Now I move different.

I do not expect anyone to be loyal to me.

I just watch how they move when things get quiet.

Because in survival, silence always tells the truth.

Chapter Ten: Family Ties

Family is supposed to be your first safety.

For me it was my first battlefield.

The word family always felt heavy in my mouth.

It meant love and violence in the same breath.

It meant being told I was cared for by the same hands that hurt me.

It meant learning that loyalty does not always mean protection.

I was raised around people who loved me the only way they knew how, which was survival.

Everyone was fighting their own demons, no one had time to learn how to love without hurting.

I watched addiction, control, and silence build the walls of our home.
It was not peace. It was just a pause between storms.

I learned early that family can break you and still call it love.
That blood can make you related but not connected.
That forgiveness becomes a habit when apology never comes.

When I left home, I thought I was running away from them.
I did not realize I was carrying them inside me.
The same anger. The same patterns. The same hunger for love in all the wrong places.
You do not escape your blood. You just learn to stop bleeding for it.

On the streets, family looks different.
It is the girl who splits her last cigarette with you.
The guy who keeps watch while you crash for an hour.
The dealer who gives you a free hit when he knows you are sick.
It is not love in the way people picture it.
It is loyalty born from pain.
There were people I called brother who would have fought for me without question.
People who would have gone to jail rather than see me fall. But there were also people who would sell me out for fifty dollars or a favor.
You never really know which one you are standing next to until the fire starts.

I have been the caretaker and the problem.
The protector and the reason for worry.
I have been the one people cried over and the one they cursed for leaving.

Family ties twist like that.
No one is only one thing in the story.

There were moments I tried to fix what was broken.
I wanted to believe that love could make it right.
But sometimes the healthiest thing you can do is stop trying to heal people who refuse to see their own wounds. You cannot build peace with people who are still at war with themselves.

The truth is I still crave family.
I still want that table where everyone laughs and no one is afraid.
But I have learned that family is not always who you are born to.
Sometimes it is the ones who show up when you have nothing left to give.
Sometimes it is the ones who see your scars and do not flinch.
Sometimes it is the ones who tell you the truth even when it hurts.

I carry both families in me.
The one that broke me and the one that helped me rebuild.
Both made me who I am.
Both taught me the price of love.

And even after everything, I still believe in family.
But now I know it is something you build, not something you inherit.

"When blood fails you, the system waits for you.
And both ask for loyalty you can't afford to give."

Chapter Eleven: The System

The system does not fix broken people. It manages them.

It keeps you in line just enough to call it order.

It punishes you for surviving the way it failed to protect you. It gives speeches about justice while building cages out of paperwork.

I have met the system in every form it wears.

Police lights flashing in my face.

Courtrooms that smell like bleach and fear.

Social workers with soft voices and cold eyes.

Rehab centers that care more about compliance than healing. Shelters that hand you a bed and take your dignity in the same breath.

The system speaks in circles.

It tells you that you are free while reminding you of your record. It tells you to get help while cutting the programs that could actually save you.

It tells you to trust while writing reports about your failures.

I have sat across from workers who smiled at my pain like it was data.

They asked about trauma like it was gossip. They handed me pamphlets about recovery and called it compassion.

They wrote my life down in files that other people would read like stories.

I remember being in court with my head down, the room full of people judging pieces of me they would never live through.

They talked about my choices like they were random.

They did not see the nights I stayed alive without food.

They did not see the bruises I hid or the people I buried. They only saw the paperwork.

The system never asks why.

It just wants who, what, where, when.
It wants your confession, not your story. It
wants your signature, not your truth.

I have been a number, a file, a statistic.
I have had my name called like I was a case, not a person. I have
seen mothers lose their children because they were too poor to
prove they were stable.
I have seen men go back to jail for missing one appointment
because the bus never came.

The system calls it rehabilitation, but it is really containment.
They do not teach you how to heal.
They teach you how to comply.
They do not care if you are better, only if you behave.

I have watched people walk out of jail and go straight back to the
streets because no one met them at the gate.
No job. No home. No plan.
Just a piece of paper that says "released" and a world that says
"you do not belong here."

And when they end up back inside, the system shakes its head like
it is surprised.
But it is not surprise. It is design.
Because chaos keeps the lights on.
Pain keeps the payroll running.
Every relapse, every re-arrest, every lost soul is another box ticked.

The system pretends to hate the streets, but they feed each other.
One makes the rules, the other breaks them, and both stay alive
from the same cycle.

I learned to play the system like it played me. I learned the language.
I learned when to cry and when to stay quiet.
I learned how to make my story sound small enough that they would let me go.
The system taught me patience and strategy.
It taught me how to hide truth in plain sight.
It taught me that survival is not always rebellion. Sometimes it is performance.

But what the system will never understand is this.
You cannot cage a soul forever.
You can document it, punish it, drug it, and bury it in files. But eventually, it finds a way to rise.

And that is what the system fears most.
People like me who learn how to play by the rules just long enough to write new ones

Chapter Twelve: Doing Time in the Cell

 I have never done long jail.
Thirty days. Weekends only.
In on Friday, out on Sunday night.
But I have known a lot of people who have done real time.
Friends who spent years behind those walls.
They gave me stories, lessons, warnings, and truths that most people on the outside will never understand.
So what I write here is not from fantasy. It is from a place of witness. From what I lived, and from what I listened to.

There are two kinds of time.
The kind the clock keeps.
And the kind your mind keeps when the clock stops mattering.
Jail is where both kinds meet.

People talk about jail like it is a lesson.
It is not.
It is a pause that stretches until it becomes a lifetime.
You sit there while the world keeps moving, and the sound of other
people's lives becomes louder than your own.

In the streets you learn movement.
In the cell you learn stillness.
And stillness can break a person faster than violence ever could.

Doing time is not just counting days.
It is learning the shape of your own thoughts.
It is hearing your past play on repeat with nowhere to run from it.
You start noticing the smallest things, like how light hits the wall or
how footsteps echo from down the hall.
Every sound becomes something to measure time by.

Some people came in wild and left quiet.
I saw that silence settle into them like a second skin.
Others came in quiet and left hollow, like they had been scraped
out.
Some never really left at all, even when the door opened.
Because the real bars are the ones you start carrying inside you.

They call it corrections, but there is nothing corrected about it.
I saw people who already knew how to survive chaos trapped in
silence.
I saw people who never felt safe locked in cages where safety did
not exist.
People who needed healing were given time instead.

But time does not heal in there.
It hardens.
It carves you out until all that is left is control and memory.

You start building rituals.
Fold your blanket a certain way.
Eat fast.
Count the steps from bed to wall.
Even in a few weekends, I felt it. Routine becomes a kind of religion. It gives you something to hold onto.

I heard stories about how some people could tell who was coming just by their footsteps.
How they learned to spot danger without moving their head.
How silence became safer than honesty.
You adapt to survive, even if it means shrinking yourself to fit the space you were never meant to belong in.

Behind the glass, the world looks smaller.
I met people waiting for visits that never came.
They would talk about how family visits become awkward, then painful, then rare.
People promise they will be there, but life keeps moving without you.
Some memorize faces because they know they might not see them again.

There were days I felt more human in a cell than I did outside.
Because at least in there no one pretended to be anything else.
Pain was visible.
Regret was normal.
Truth was currency.

The hardest part of jail is not the noise or the rules.
It is the waiting.

Waiting for letters that do not come.
Waiting for names to be called.
Waiting to feel like yourself again.
I saw people break without making a sound.
People who looked strong on the streets cried into pillows when the lights went out.
And some found peace in that same silence, not because it healed them but because it forced them to face their ghosts until they stopped running.

Jail changes you.
Not because it teaches you right from wrong, but because it teaches you how to survive a world that no longer believes you can change.

When I got out, the air felt fake.
Freedom felt too big.
I still folded my blanket.
I still ate fast.
I still woke up waiting for someone to yell count.

Doing time does not end when you walk out the gate.
It follows you.
It lives in how you watch people, how you measure space, how you breathe.
Jail does not end.
It just changes shape.
And once you have lived inside the cell, you never stop trying to prove you belong outside it.

Chapter Thirteen: The Hustler's Mind

The hustler's mind is not built for peace.
It is wired for motion.
It is trained to read energy faster than people can speak.
It calculates risk, reward, and escape in the same breath.

When you live by survival, your brain becomes a weapon.
Every sense sharpens.
Every glance becomes data.
Every silence becomes threat or opportunity.
I learned how to watch people the way other kids watched cartoons.
How they shifted when they lied.
How their tone changed when money came up.
How their eyes moved when they were hiding something. You learn to read people before they read you because being wrong could cost you everything.

The hustler's mind is a mix of fear and genius.
You can think ten steps ahead and still be trapped in the same place.
You can make money from nothing but still be broke inside.
It is strategy without rest. Survival
without pause.

I have lied with precision.
I have charmed people I could not stand.
I have built trust I planned to break before they did it to me first.
It was not cruelty. It was defense.
The streets do not reward honesty. They
reward results.

You become addicted to control.
Not because you want power, but because chaos taught you how it feels to have none.
You start planning everything.
You start watching everyone.
You trust your paranoia more than your peace.

There were nights when I felt invincible.
The rush of a deal done right.
The phone buzzing non-stop.
Money coming fast and easy.
It feels like freedom until you realize it is just another leash with prettier chains.

The hustler's mind believes everything can be fixed if you move fast enough.
You run on adrenaline until you forget what calm feels like. And when you finally slow down, your thoughts start chasing you.
That is when the fear creeps back in.
That is when you remember why you started running in the first place.

I used to think I was smarter than everyone.
That I could play both sides and stay untouched.
But every game has a cost.
You cannot outsmart the pain forever.
It will always find a new way to collect.

The hustler's mind is built on survival logic.
Never owe.
Never need.
Never trust too deep.

Always have a plan B, and a plan C hidden behind it.
Always know the exits.
Always keep something they cannot take from you.

I used to think this mindset made me strong.
Now I see it made me tired.
There is no rest in always being ready.
There is no joy in winning a game that never ends.

But even now, I cannot unlearn it.
The hustle trained me to see the world like a chessboard.
Every person a move. Every risk a calculation.
Even when I am safe, I still scan for danger. Even
when I am home, I still sleep light.

The hustler's mind does not forget.
It adapts.
It evolves.
It survives.
And no matter how far I go from the streets, that part of me still
wakes up first.

Chapter Fourteen: The Women in the Game

The women in the game walk a line so thin it cuts.
We are expected to be soft and ruthless at the same time.
We are the backbone and the blame.
We make the money, keep the secrets, take the fall, and still get
called weak.

Every woman in the life learns the same lesson.
Power is not given. It is taken.

And the moment you take it, they start plotting to take it back.

I have seen women who could run circles around men twice their age and still be treated like they were lucky to be in the room.
I have seen women make more money than their bosses and still get paid in promises.
The game loves to use our beauty, our loyalty, our pain, and then tell us we asked for it.

I learned early that if you want respect, you have to walk like you already have it.
Eyes up. Voice steady.
Never show fear, never show need.
You dress like armor, talk like business, and move like no one owns you.

But under that strength there is always the cost.
The looks that turn into threats.
The touches that come with conditions.
The way men call you queen one minute and problem the next. The way you start believing that love and loyalty are earned through

suffering.

I have been the pretty one in a room full of wolves. I have been protected, used, praised, and punished for the same thing.
I have smiled when I wanted to scream.
I have played dumb so I could stay alive.

The women in the game are chameleons.
We can shift faster than anyone.
We know how to blend in, how to charm, how to disappear.

We are survivors in heels and hustlers in hoodies. We
carry grief like jewelry.

I remember the girls who did not make it.
The ones who got caught in the wrong car, the wrong house, the
wrong deal.
Their names still sit heavy in my chest.
No one puts them on posters or murals.
The world forgets women like us unless we die beautifully.

There were women who mothered me when I did not have one.
They taught me how to stay safe, how to spot a setup, how to hide
my fear behind eyeliner.
They taught me that survival has a sisterhood, even when no one
else understands it.

We took care of each other in ways the world never did. Shared
clothes. Shared secrets. Shared warnings about men who smiled
too wide.
It was not perfect, but it was real.
We were a family built from broken glass and late-night rides.

Being a woman in the game means knowing your worth and
pretending you do not.
It means using your softness as a weapon and praying it does not
backfire.
It means loving people who see you as a resource and calling it
connection.

The game sells dreams.
To women, it sells the idea that we can be both untouchable and
desired.
But no one tells you how exhausting that is.
How heavy it feels to be wanted but never safe.

I have met women who ran the streets like generals. I have
met women who sold their pain for survival and then used that
same pain to build empires.

We are not weak. We are not lost.

We are the proof that even in the darkest corners, strength can wear
lipstick.

The women in the game are both the story and the secret. We are
the ones the world judges the hardest and understands the least.

We are the proof that survival is not just something men do. We
are the reason the game keeps going, and sometimes, the reason it
changes.

Chapter Fifteen: Violence and Power

Violence is the first language I ever learned fluently.

It speaks louder than apology.

It settles arguments when words do not work. It
builds fear, and fear becomes power.

The streets do not ask if you like violence.

They ask if you can survive it.

They ask if you can give it back when it comes for you.

I used to think power meant being the one who hit first.

Being the one who never cried.

Being the one no one dared to touch.

But real power is quieter than that.

It is knowing you could destroy something and choosing not to. It
is walking away when everyone expects you to burn it down.

There were nights when I saw things that still wake me up.

Fists, knives, guns, screams.
People I cared about bleeding while pretending it was nothing.
You learn to stay calm in the chaos.
You learn to clean blood like it is part of the job. You learn
that shaking hands can still aim straight when you are scared
enough.

Violence does not just live in the streets.
It lives in relationships, in homes, in systems.
It wears perfume and smiles for pictures.
It hides behind the word discipline.
It shows up in how people talk to you after they break you.

I have been hit, pushed, pinned, and silenced.
I have hit back too.
Because survival does not care about right and wrong. It
only cares about who is still standing when it ends.

Power and violence feed each other.
The more power you have, the more violence you can hide.
The more violence you take, the more power you crave.
It becomes a loop that eats your humanity one bite at a time.

There was a time when I thought I needed to be feared.
It felt safer than being loved.
Fear meant control.
Love meant risk.
Fear kept people in line. Love
let them too close.

But fear is lonely.
You cannot build a life out of intimidation.
You can win the room and still lose your soul.

I have seen men who needed violence to feel alive. I have
seen women who used it to protect what was left of them.
I have seen children who grew up thinking pain was proof of love.
That is how the cycle keeps spinning.

Power is not what the streets taught me.
It is what surviving them taught me.
It is the ability to stand in front of the same world that tried to
destroy you and not flinch.
It is the calm that comes after you have lost everything and still
breathe steady.

Violence built my armor.
But it also stole parts of me I will never get back.
It made me strong, but it also made me numb.
It taught me how to fight, but it took away my reason to.

Real power is not in fear.
It is in restraint.
It is in knowing you could burn it all down but choosing to build
something instead.
And sometimes, that choice is the hardest fight of all.

Chapter Sixteen: The Price of Respect

Respect is the most expensive thing in the streets.
It costs more than drugs.
More than love.
More than freedom.
Everyone says they want respect, but most do not survive what it
takes to get it.

The game teaches you that fear and respect look the same from a distance.
If they do not love you, make them fear you.
If they fear you, they will not cross you. That
is the logic we live by.

I learned that lesson young.
When people stop seeing you as a victim, they start leaving you alone.
When your eyes harden and your voice stays calm in chaos, people listen differently.
Power makes noise, but respect is silent.

You do not earn respect with words.
You earn it with consistency.
You show up when you say you will.
You pay what you owe.
You keep your mouth shut when silence could save a life. You never beg, never fold, never snitch.

But the price of that kind of respect is high.
You start losing pieces of yourself just to keep the image intact.
You stop crying even when you need to.
You stop laughing because joy looks like weakness. You start playing a character that becomes harder to take off every year.

There were times I had to remind people who I was.
Not because I wanted violence, but because the streets test everyone eventually. Rumors travel faster than truth.
If you do not defend your name, someone else will rewrite it for you.

Reputation becomes survival.

You can have nothing in your pockets, but if your name still holds weight, you will eat.
Your word becomes your currency. One lie and you are broke forever.

I have seen people die over respect.
Arguments that turned into funerals.
Friendships that ended over pride.
No one wants to look weak, even when being alive would have been the smarter choice.

The truth is, respect in the streets is not about morals.
It is about image.
How you move, how you react, how long you can keep control. It is exhausting pretending you do not care about anything when everything inside you is screaming.

There were days I wished I could just be soft again.
To not have to prove myself every time I walked into a room.
To not have to keep my voice low and my hands ready. But softness is a luxury survival does not allow.

The price of respect is isolation.
People stop getting close because they cannot tell if you are safe or dangerous.
You become both.
You start to like the distance because it feels like protection. But it is really loneliness wearing armor.

I have been respected by people who never loved me.
I have been feared by people who never knew me.
And when the lights went out, none of it kept me warm.

The kind of respect that matters now is different.

It is the kind that does not need to be performed.
It is the kind that lives in silence.
The kind you give yourself when you wake up and still choose to keep going.

Because surviving without losing yourself is the deepest kind of respect there is.

Chapter Seventeen: Trust Issues

Trust is a language I never learned to speak fluently. Every time I thought I understood it, someone changed the meaning.

In the streets, trust is currency.
You spend it carefully and never get a refund.
You do not trust words. You trust patterns.
You do not trust smiles. You trust silence. You do not trust time. You trust results.

I learned to read people like maps because getting lost could kill you.
I watched how they breathed when they lied.
I paid attention to what they did when no one was looking. You do not ask for honesty. You observe it.

The truth is, survival turns everyone into a liar in some way.
We lie to stay safe.
We lie to keep eating.
We lie to keep control.
Even the honest ones learn how to bend truth just enough to make it through.

I trusted people who broke me and doubted people who cared. Because in my world, love came with an agenda and kindness always had a catch.

If someone was too nice, I wondered what they wanted. If they did not want anything, I wondered when they would leave.

Trust issues are not paranoia. They are protection.

They are the body's way of saying, I remember what happened last time.

And when last time almost killed you, your instincts stop giving people chances.

I have slept beside danger and felt safer than I did with family. I have trusted strangers with my secrets and lied to people who tried to save me.

Because in the survival lifestyle, trust is not about honesty.

It is about strategy.

You trust people for what they can do, not who they are.

There were moments when I tested people on purpose.

Pushed them away just to see if they would stay.

Started fights just to see if they would hit back or walk away. That is what trauma does. It makes you rehearse the pain so it does not surprise you again.

I do not trust easy, but I am loyal to a fault.

Once I let you in, I will fight for you like family.

I will defend your name like it is mine.

But if you ever betray me, you are gone forever.

No warnings, no second chances. That is how you learn to survive.

The hardest person to trust has always been myself. Because when you have lived through chaos, peace feels suspicious. When things go right, you start waiting for the wrong. When people love you, you question why.

I have doubted my own good days.
Sabotaged moments that felt too calm.
Because I did not know how to exist without danger.
I did not know how to trust happiness when I was used to pain.

Trust issues do not fade. They evolve.
You start learning who deserves access and who only deserves observation.
You start trusting actions over explanations.
You stop trying to prove yourself to people who do not deserve the truth.

I do not need to trust everyone anymore.
I just need to trust that I will survive whoever they turn out to be.

Chapter Eighteen: The Code

Every world has rules.
Ours just were not written down.
The code is not in a book or a law.
It lives in your chest.
You learn it by watching who makes it home and who does not.

The code says loyalty first.
Never talk.
Never snitch.
Never steal from family.

Never show fear in public.
Never forget who fed you when you were hungry.

The code sounds simple until you live it.
Until you have to choose between freedom and silence.
Between your conscience and your crew.
Between your own heartbeat and someone else's name.

I grew up memorizing the code before I even knew what integrity meant.
It was how we stayed alive.
How we found belonging when the world called us lost. It was family, honor, law, and religion all rolled into one.

You do not question the code when you are in it.
You just follow it.
You learn when to speak, when to disappear, when to take the fall.
Because in survival, your word is the only currency that never loses value.

I have seen people break the code for money.
For fear.
For love.
For deals that promised freedom and delivered more chains.
And every time someone folds, the air changes. The trust dies fast, and the streets remember longer than the people do.

The code is not fair.
It protects killers and punishes kindness.
It rewards silence even when silence means letting injustice win.
It asks you to bleed for people who would not visit you in jail. But you follow it because the alternative is being nothing.

I carried that code like a religion.

I lived by it even after I left the game.
It shaped how I loved, how I spoke, how I trusted.
I still struggle to break it in places it does not belong.
Still struggle to ask for help.
Still stay quiet when I should speak.

The code becomes instinct.
You start keeping secrets from people who are not even asking questions.
You start walking with your back to the wall.
You start scanning exits out of habit.
It becomes part of who you are, even when you do not want it to be.

There was a time I broke the code.
Not for greed, not for fear, but for freedom.
Because sometimes keeping the code means dying with your truth still caged.
And I had already buried too much of myself.

Breaking it did not make me weak.
It made me real.
Because codes are meant to protect people, not erase them. And I realized I did not owe silence to a world that had already stolen my voice.

The code gave me structure when I had none.
It gave me belonging when family failed.
It gave me identity when I did not know who I was. But it also taught me how to hide behind loyalty even when it was killing me.

I still respect the code.

It saved my life.
But I also learned that loyalty means nothing if it costs your soul.
There is honor in survival, but there is also honor in honesty. And
the strongest thing I ever did was rewrite the code for myself.

Chapter Nineteen: The Fall

There are parts of this story that sound like

they are about jail.
And they are.
But the truth is, that was only the surface of it.
The cell was never just a place. It was a mirror.
It was the best way I knew how to explain what

falling felt like.
Because sometimes the real prison is not built

from walls or guards or bars.

It is built from choices, losses, grief, and moments

when you stop recognizing yourself.
So when I talk about jail, I am also talking about life,

about consequence, about collapse, about the kind of

fall that forces you to face what you have

 been running from.

This is the only way I know how to tell it.
Not perfectly, but honestly.

Every hustle ends the same way.
Fast money turns slow.
Loyalty turns thin.
And the walls start closing in.

The fall never happens all at once.
It creeps in like smoke under a door.
One bad call. One night too long. One deal that feels off but you take it anyway because you are running out of options. You tell yourself you still got it, but the game is already moving without you.

I felt it before I saw it.
The silence after the calls stopped coming.
The eyes that looked away when I walked in.
The whispers that sounded like goodbye.
That is when I knew my time was running out.

The streets have no retirement plan.
You either get out clean, get caught, or get buried.
And clean never really means clean.
Because even when you make it out, the memories follow.

My fall came slow at first.
I was tired. I was high. I was trying to keep the illusion alive while my world was cracking underneath.
People thought I was still winning.
They saw the clothes, the money, the smile.
They did not see the sleepless nights, the paranoia, the shaking hands counting cash that already felt cursed.
Then came the day everything stopped.
One knock at the door that was too loud.

One name I never thought would fold.

One lie that became a record.

The kind of moment you never forget because it rewires who you are.

I remember the sound of the cuffs.

Cold metal, loud room, my own heartbeat in my ears.

It was not anger I felt. It was clarity.

The game was over and I was not the one who won.

A cell is not just a place.

It is a mirror.

It shows you every choice you made, every person you hurt, every part of yourself you tried to bury.

You start to see who was real and who was just real enough.

The first night in that cell was quiet in a way that terrified me.

No noise to drown out the truth.

No chaos to hide behind.

Just me and the echo of everything I had been running from.

That is when the mask cracked.

When I realized I did not even know who I was without the hustle.

The streets had raised me, but they never taught me how to stop running.

The fall is not failure.

It is exposure.

It strips away everything that is not real.

The lies. The pride. The illusions of control.

Until all that is left is the raw truth of who you are and what you have done.

I have seen people break in that place.

Cry, scream, lose their minds.

I did not cry. I sat still.

I let the silence swallow me.

Because for the first time, I did not have to pretend.

The fall hurts because it shows you what survival costs.

You realize how much of yourself you traded just to stay alive.

And once you see that, you can never go back.

The fall was not the end of me.

It was the first time I stood still long enough to see what I had become.

It was the moment I stopped being untouchable and started being real.

And real, I learned, is harder than the streets ever were.

"You think falling is the end.

Until you realize the floor has another floor beneath it."

Chapter Twenty: Rock Bottom

People talk about rock bottom like it is one place. Like it is a single moment when everything breaks and then somehow you rise again.

That is a lie.

There is rock bottom.

And then there is rock bottom's basement.

Rock bottom is when you lose everything.

Rock bottom's basement is when you stop caring that you did.

The first time I hit bottom, I thought that was it.
I had no money, no home, no friends who would answer, no body left to use for comfort.
I was sitting on a floor that did not belong to me, shaking, hungry, high, and hollow.
But I was still breathing.
And that meant there was still further to fall.

Rock bottom is pain.
Rock bottom's basement is numb.
It is when the world could burn down around you and you would not even flinch.
It is when death feels like relief, not fear.

I remember that basement.
The one that was not always a place but a state of mind.
I could hear people living outside. Cars, laughter, normal.
But I was not part of it anymore.
It was like watching life from underwater.

People say hitting bottom is where change begins. They never tell you how long you can live down there before you remember what up feels like.

Down there, the air is heavy.
The mirrors lie.
Time does not pass.
Every day feels like the same day you swore would be your last.
You make deals with yourself you never keep.
You promise to get clean, to call someone, to eat. But then the numb wins again.

Rock bottom's basement is when you stop even pretending you are okay.
You stop lying to yourself.
You stop trying to play strong.
You sit in the wreckage and realize no one is coming.
Not the system. Not family. Not God.
Just you and whatever is left of your soul.

I have seen people die in that place with their eyes open.
Still chasing a feeling that was never coming back. Still waiting for a second chance they would not take even if it arrived.
And I have been one of them.

The scariest part of rock bottom's basement is how peaceful it feels.
No more pressure. No more expectations.
You accept that this is your life now.
That maybe survival was the punishment, not the blessing.

But somewhere in that stillness, something small starts whispering.
Not hope exactly. Just defiance.
The voice that says not yet.
The same one that kept me alive when I should not have been. It does not ask you to believe. It just asks you to move.

That whisper is the line between dying and living again.
Between giving up and giving in.
It is not a scream. It is not dramatic. It
is quiet. Simple. True.

Rock bottom shows you who you are.
Rock bottom's basement shows you what you are made of. And when you finally start climbing out, you do it without pretending.

No pride. No mask. No lies.
Just the truth that somehow, against every reason, you are still here.

And sometimes that alone is the miracle.

Chapter TwentyOne: Climbing Out

Climbing out is not a clean story.
It is not a sunrise moment or a movie scene with music in the background.
It is ugly.
It is slow.
It is you against everything you built to protect yourself.

People think climbing out starts with hope.
It doesn't.
It starts with exhaustion.
You get tired of dying.
You get tired of watching the same day on repeat. You get tired of being your own ghost.

There was no one waiting with a plan for me.
No therapist in a white room.
No friend with a car outside.
Just a decision I could barely make.
Either keep going down or start crawling up.

At first, the climb is small.
You eat something real.
You shower.
You answer one message.

You tell one truth.
You stop lying about being fine.
And then you do it again tomorrow.
It does not look like progress, but it is.

When you live in survival long enough, peace feels wrong.
So even when you start getting better, your body fights it.
You jump at kindness.
You wait for the catch.
You sabotage the good because bad feels familiar.

Climbing out means rewiring your instincts one day at a time. You start noticing the difference between real danger and memory.
You start realizing that not every loud voice means harm. You start learning how to exist without always preparing for war.

I have fallen more times than I have climbed.
Some days I made it two steps up and slid ten steps down.
But even sliding down means you are still moving.
And that is what survival looks like when you stop pretending.

The truth is, no one tells you how hard it is to live after you stop dying.
You have to build a new way to think, a new way to breathe, a new way to want.
You have to meet yourself for the first time without all the noise.
And sometimes that silence hurts worse than the chaos ever did.

There were moments I almost went back.
The game calls you when it knows you are weak. The streets whisper your name when they feel you pulling away.
They promise comfort, familiarity, control.
But it is all illusion.

You can't go back to who you were because that person died to keep you alive.

The climb is lonely.
No one celebrates the quiet victories.
No one claps when you choose water over whiskey, or peace over chaos.
But those are the real wins.
Those are the moments that rebuild your bones.

Every scar becomes a map of where you've been.
Every bruise becomes a lesson. Every
breath becomes proof.

The climb never really ends.
You just get stronger.
You stop looking down.
You start trusting your own footing.
And one day, without realizing it, you look around and the air feels different.
You are not at the top.
But you are not in the basement anymore either.

You are somewhere in between.
Still climbing.
Still breathing. Still
alive.

And for the first time, that is enough.

Chapter TwentyTwo: Ghosts of the Past

The past does not stay buried.

It lingers.

It breathes.

It follows you into every quiet room and every dream that feels too real.

People think once you climb out you are free.

But freedom does not erase memory.

You carry ghosts in your blood.

You hear their voices in songs, in sirens, in the silence before sleep.

Some ghosts wear faces.

Old friends, old enemies, old versions of me.

Some died on the streets.

Some are still alive but gone anyway.

Some live only in the parts of me that refuse to die.

I can still smell the places I swore I would never go back to.

Basements, alleys, motel rooms with curtains that never opened.

I can still hear the sound of certain names.

The tone that meant danger before I even turned around. The echo of laughter that always came before loss.

The ghosts do not want revenge.

They want attention.

They want to remind you who you were.

They whisper when you are happy.

They show up when you feel safe.

They say, remember me, like memory is a chain instead of a story.

Sometimes I still wake up ready to run.

Heart pounding.
Body tense.
Like I am back in a room that no longer exists.
The mind does not care that the danger is gone. It
only remembers how it felt to survive it.

I have tried to outrun the past.
Drugs could not do it.
Distance could not do it.
Love could not do it.
Because you cannot run from something that lives inside you.

There were people I hurt who never forgave me.
People who hurt me who never said sorry.
I used to think closure meant getting answers. Now I
know it just means accepting silence.

The hardest ghost to face is the one that looks like you.
The one that remembers every lie you told to stay alive.
The one that asks, who are you without the fight. Sometimes I
still do not know how to answer.

The ghosts of the past are not always curses.
Some are teachers.
They remind me where I came from.
They remind me what I survived.
They keep me honest when the world starts pretending pain never
existed.

I still talk to them sometimes.
Not out loud, just in thought.
I tell them thank you for keeping me alive.

But I also tell them I am done carrying them. Because
ghosts do not belong in the future.

The past built me.
But it does not own me.
I walk with my ghosts now instead of running from them.
I let them remind me, not define me.
Because every ghost that follows me is proof of a story that did
not end when it should have. And I am still here to tell it.

Coming Soon

The Survival Handbook A Manual for the Survival Parent

Parenting is hard enough when life has been kind to you.
But when you are parenting through survival, it is a different kind
of battle.
It is trying to raise soft children when the world has hardened you.

It is trying to teach trust when you learned to survive without it.
It is showing love while still learning what love even feels like in safety.

The Survival Handbook A Manual for the Survival Parent is for those of us who are breaking cycles we never signed up to repeat.
It is for the mothers and fathers who are healing while raising.
For the parents who have lived through trauma, addiction, violence, or chaos, and are now learning how to guide small souls while still rebuilding their own.

This book does not come from perfection.
It comes from truth.
It is about learning to parent yourself while parenting them.
It is about mistakes, repair, growth, and grace.
It is about surviving parenthood in a world that never taught you safety, and creating safety anyway.

Because survival does not end when you have children.
It just changes shape.
And this time, you get to choose what grows from it.

About the Author

Arya Skyee is a survivor, writer, and advocate who turned a lifetime of lived experience into testimony.
She writes not from theory but from the streets, the shelters, the cells, and the silence that shaped her.

As the founder of T.R.U.E Love Foundation, Arya has dedicated her life to creating spaces where survivors of addiction, abuse, and poverty are no longer defined by what they endured but by what they have become. Through her work in advocacy, education, and social justice, she continues to challenge systems that punish survival instead of understanding it.

The Survival Handbook: A Manual for the Survival Lifestyle is her rawest work, a chronicle of truth for those who have lived through the unlivable and still breathe.

Arya lives in Canada where she continues to write, create, and build community spaces for empowerment and transformation through T.R.U.E Love Foundation.

Learn more at www.truelovefoundation.ca